Watching the Weather

Wind

Elizabeth Miles

Heinemann Library
Chicago, Illinois

Designed by Richard Parker and Q2A Solutions
Illustrations: Jeff Edwards
Originated by Dot Gradations Ltd.
Printed and bound in China by South China Printing Company

09 08 07 06 05
10 9 8 7 6 5 4 3 2 1

Library of Congress Cataloging-in-Publication Data
Miles, Elizabeth, 1960-
    Wind / Elizabeth Miles.
       p. cm. -- (Watching the weather)
    Includes bibliographical references and index.
    ISBN 1-4034-6550-9 -- ISBN 1-4034-6555-X (pbk.)
1. Winds--Juvenile literature. I. Title. II. Series.
    QC931.4.M55 2005
    551.51'8--dc22
                            2004018483

Acknowledgments
The Publishers would like to thank the following for permission to reproduce photographs: Alamy p.**7** (Neil Setchfield); Corbis pp. **9**, **13**, **14** (Jim Sugar), **22** (Jim Reed), **23**, **24**, **25** (Jim Reed), **26**, **27**; Getty Images pp.**8** (PhotoDisc), **12**(Taxi/D Sim); Panos p. **21** (Clive Shirley); PA Photos p. **17** (EPA); Photolibrary.com p. **15** (Warwick Kent); PhotoDisc p.**5**; Reuters pp. **18** (Sherwin Crasto), **19** (Fatih Saribas); Rex Features pp. **4** (IJO), **20** (EDPPICS /SFinlay); Tudor Photography pp. **10**, **28**, **29**.

Cover photograph of palm trees blowing in a gale reproduced with permission of Getty Images/Taxi.

The Publishers would like to thank Daniel Ogden for his assistance in the preparation of this book.

Every effort has been made to contact copyright holders of any material reproduced in this book. Any omissions will be rectified in subsequent printings if notice is given to the Publisher.

Contents

Some words are shown in bold, **like this**. You can find out what they mean by looking in the glossary.

What Is Wind?

Wind is moving air. Outside, on a windy day, you can feel the air blowing against your face.

You cannot see the wind, but you can feel it push against you.

4

Wind pushes things along. It blows clouds across the sky and sailing boats across the sea. Winds can be fast or slow. They can feel strong or gentle.

People fly kites using the wind.

Why Do Winds Blow?

Winds blow because the sun heats the earth. Then the earth warms the air above. When the warm air rises, cool air rushes in to take its place.

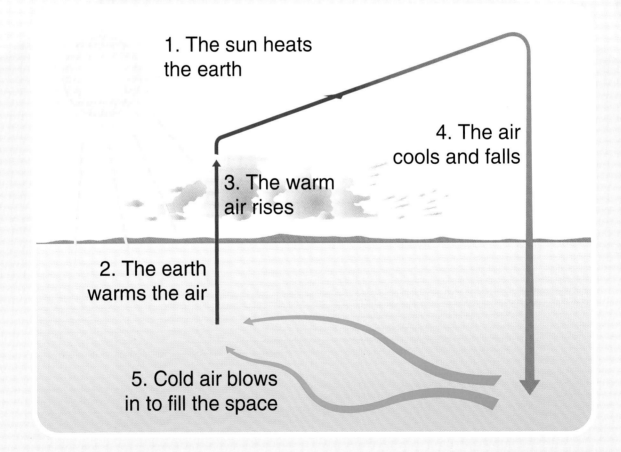

1. The sun heats the earth

4. The air cools and falls

3. The warm air rises

2. The earth warms the air

5. Cold air blows in to fill the space

A cool wind blowing in from the sea is sometimes called a sea **breeze**.

Some winds feel warm and some feel cool. When the land is warmer than the sea, cool winds can blow in from the sea.

Wind Speed

Winds move at different speeds. Slower, gentler winds are called **breezes**. Faster, stronger winds are called **gales**. A gentle breeze blows only small or light things about.

Flags flutter in a gentle breeze.

A fast wind pushes a sailing boat along and can help it win a race.

A fast wind can be helpful or dangerous. Very fast winds can be so strong that they can push cars over and damage buildings.

Measuring Wind

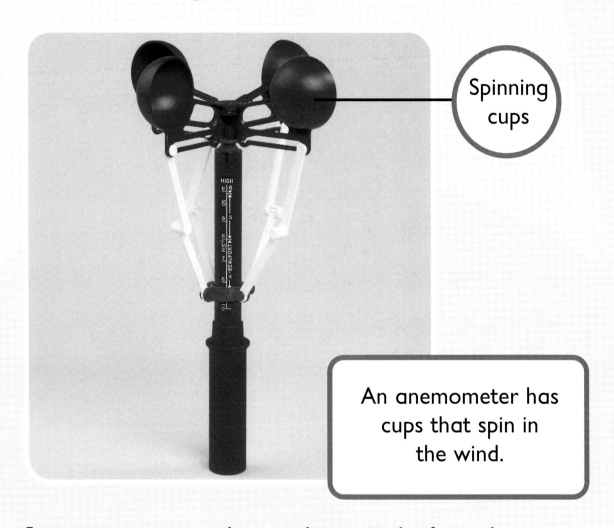

Spinning cups

An anemometer has cups that spin in the wind.

It is important to know the speed of wind. The faster the wind is, the more damage it can do. An **anemometer** is used to measure wind speed.

Francis Beaufort gave a list of names and numbers to winds of different strengths. It is called the Beaufort Scale. You can also use it to guess wind speeds.

The Beaufort Scale			
Force	Speed	Description	Picture
1 Light air	1–5 km/h (1–3 mph)	Smoke shows the wind direction	
3 Gentle **breeze**	12–19 km/h (8–12 mph)	Loose paper blows around	
5 Fresh breeze	30–39 km/h (19–24 mph)	Leaves are blown off trees	
8 **Gale**	62–74 km/h (39–46 mph)	Twigs are broken from trees	
10 Storm	88–102 km/h (55–63 mph)	Trees are blown over	

Winds and Storms

Powerful winds blow in a storm. During a storm, winds may blow down **power lines** and lift off the roofs of houses.

Strong winds at sea can create high waves.

Wind faster than 73 miles per hour (117 kilometers per hour) is called a hurricane.

The most dangerous storms are **hurricanes** and **tornadoes**. These bring winds that can pull up trees and blow down houses.

Wind Direction

This **weather vane** shows the wind is blowing from the south.

Weather **forecasters** study wind direction to find out where the wind is blowing from. This helps them figure out what kind of weather is coming.

People flying
airplanes need to
know the wind
direction.
Windsocks show
the wind direction
at airports. They
point in the
direction the wind
is blowing.

Windsocks help people
fly airplanes safely.

Winds Around the World

Some winds blow for short distances and last only a few hours. Other winds blow across longer distances and last for many weeks. We name winds after the direction they come from.

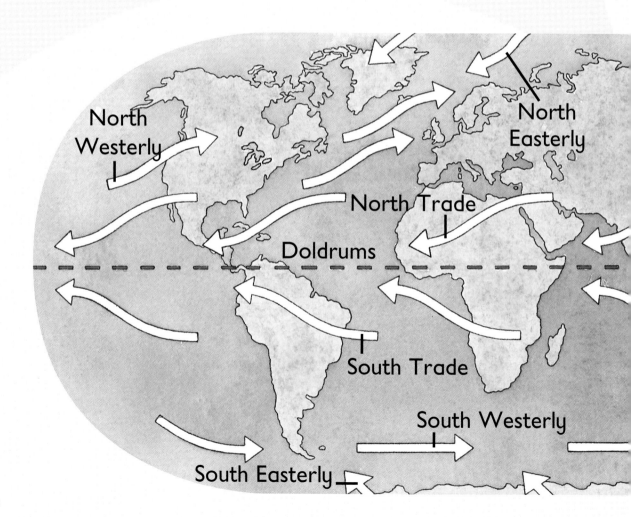

North Westerly

North Easterly

North Trade

Doldrums

South Trade

South Westerly

South Easterly

Jet stream winds can push airplanes and hot air balloons along faster.

Jet streams are fast winds that blow high up in the sky. Jet streams can blow across very long distances at speeds much faster than a car can travel.

Winds and the Seasons

Different winds blow in different seasons. In some places during summer, **monsoon** winds blow. They bring lots of rain.

Monsoon winds can bring lots of rain, which helps **crops** grow.

Winter winds can bring icy weather to places where it is often warmer. The winds can bring freezing **temperatures** and snowstorms.

In winter, cold winds can cause snowstorms called **blizzards**.

Wind and Plants

After a storm, fallen trees may block roads. Sometimes they fall on houses.

Strong winds can do lots of damage. They can even uproot trees and blow them across fields or roads.

Winds can blow soil away and damage **crops**. People put up **windbreaks** to stop the wind from damaging their plants.

A windbreak helps people protect their crops.

Wind and People

Wind can cause accidents. Powerful winds can push cars off the road or turn trucks over. Warning signs are put up along roads where there are often winds.

Winds can be strong enough to push a truck over.

Windsurfers need wind to blow them across the water.

Some winds are useful, and some can be used for fun. We can use sea winds to sail boats and to windsurf.

Disaster: Tornado

Tornadoes are one of the most dangerous kinds of weather. They are also called whirlwinds or twisters because the air inside them spins very fast.

The spinning **funnel** of a tornado stretches from a storm cloud down to the ground.

Tornadoes can lift and then drop large objects. They can even destroy houses.

Many tornadoes last only a few minutes. In that short time, they can travel a long way. A tornado can destroy almost anything in its path.

Wind Power

Windmills have been using wind power for hundreds of years. The wind pushes the sails around. The sails then turn machinery for grinding grain or moving water.

Machinery in this windmill changes grain into flour for making bread.

These wind turbines make energy that becomes electricity for towns and cities.

Wind **turbines** use the wind to make energy. They have blades that go around in the wind. The energy from the turning blades is made into **electricity**.

Project: Where is the Wind Coming From?

Find out the direction of the wind where you live. First, you will need to make a wind sock.

You will need:
- sheet of paper
- scissors
- sticky tape
- tissue paper
- paper clip
- needle and thread
- compass
- pole

1. Fold the paper over three times to make a strip.

2. Cut the tissue paper into long thin streamers.

3. Tape one end of each streamer to the strip.

4. Tape the ends of the strip together to make a narrow tube, with the streamers coming out of it.

5. Use the needle to poke four holes in the tube. Put pieces of thread through each hole. Tie all the ends of the thread together.

6. Tie the windsock to a pole with thread.

7. Use a compass to check the wind direction. Check it a few times during one day to see if it changes.

Ask a grown-up to help you.

Glossary

anemometer instrument used for measuring the speed of the wind

blizzard snowstorm with strong winds

breeze gentle wind

crop plant grown for food or to sell, such as vegetables and fruit

electricity energy that powers machinery and lights

forecaster person who figures out what the weather might be

funnel shape of a tornado. A tornado is wide at the top and thin at the bottom.

gale fast wind that can do a lot of damage

hurricane storm with very strong winds and heavy rain

monsoon summer wind that brings lots of rain

power line wire that carries electricity to where it is needed

temperature how hot or cold something is

tornado storm with winds that spin very fast

turbine machine with blades that turn very fast to make energy

More Books to Read

Ashwell, Miranda, and Owen, Andy. *What is Weather?: Wind*. Chicago: Heinemann Library, 2000.

Llewellyn, Claire. *Bright Sparks: Wild, Wet, and Windy*. New York: Walker Books, 1997.

Simon, Seymour. *Hurricanes*. New York: HarperCollins, 2003.

Index